With love to Quis – Elvis lives (see p. 70) Love, Peggy & Barry

High Notes

Fascinating Musical Instruments at the National Music Museum

A SOUVENIR BOOK

national music museum

Vermillion, South Dakota

Painted detail, back of Andrea Amati 'King' cello, mid-1500's, p. 44

High Notes: Fascinating Instruments at the National Music Museum
Vermillion, South Dakota
A Souvenir Book

Published by
National Music Museum
414 East Clark Street
Vermillion, South Dakota 57069
www.nmmusd.org

ISBN: 978-0-9848269-6-4

Editorial team:
Patricia L. Bornhofen—lead
Margaret Downie Banks
Rodger Kelly
Sabine K. Klaus
Deborah Check Reeves
Arian Sheets
Michael Suing

Color imaging by Professional Graphics, Rockford, IL

Printed in Canada by Friesens

Photographers:
Patricia Bornhofen
Dara Lohnes-Davies
Tucker Densley
Dorling Kindersley Ltd
Tony Jones
Spencer Lowell
Emanuele Marconi
Mark Olencki
Aaron Packard
Simon R. H. Spicer
Matthew Tolzmann
Bill Willroth Sr.

Civil War snare drum photo, p. 15, courtesy Cowan's Auctions, Inc., Cincinnati, Ohio

Page 1: Detail of Looßer Swiss House Organ, p. 78

Contents

Detail of Orpheus playing lyre, painted under lid of Andreas Ruckers harpsichord (p. 73)

Overture

The National Music Museum is *"one of the largest and most important collections of historical instruments in the world,"* whose *"galleries teem with masterpieces."*

—*New York Times*, September 2, 2015

In this book you will find just a *fraction* of the National Music Museum's amazing collections—some of the 'high notes.'

Like our collections overall, some of the instruments herein are fascinating for their incomparable sound quality, some for their extraordinary beauty or rarity, some for their unequalled craftsmanship and preeminent makers, some for their compelling cultural contexts or ownership histories, some for their materials and technical ingenuity, some for their associations with great performers. All are survivors, valued through time.

What we say about each instrument in this book is based on the best information we have at the present. Museum collections are works-in-progress. Each musical instrument is shrouded in some sort of mystery. New research continues to uncover new information—filling in the gaps of knowledge. We look forward to continuing to study and care for these instruments and sharing their stories with you.

Thank you to the many people who have made and are making the National Music Museum possible.

Angels with crown, symbolizing King Charles IX of France—detail from painting on the back of Andrea Amati 'King' cello (mid 1500's), one of the crown jewels of the museum **[p. 44].**

The National Music Museum mission: Explore, enjoy, and preserve the world of musical instruments.

1910 Carnegie building facade of National Music Museum, Vermillion, South Dakota

Historical High Notes
at the National Music Museum

How did the National Music Museum get started?

The National Music Museum (NMM) might not exist today had it not been for the determination of one young man to follow his passions rather than fulfill his family's expectations.

Raised to run the family farm in southern Minnesota, **Arne Baldwin Larson** (1904–1988), or "Arne B.," as he was called, was also always around music. As a boy, he played in the family orchestra and other ensembles, learning clarinet and violin, as well as any other instruments he could get his hands on. Arne B. was fascinated with how different instruments were played, but more than anything, he wanted to know what they sounded like. By collecting instruments, he could collect their sounds.

The 1920s was just the right time to collect American-made brass and woodwind instruments. After World War I, the U.S. agreed to

LEFT:
Arne B. Larson, Hanska, Minnesota, 1925

RIGHT:
Arne B. Larson with a portion of his collection in his Brookings, South Dakota, home, 1954

abide by the international pitch standard of A=440 vibrations per second. Manufacturers began producing new instrument models in this 'low pitch,' and players started selling or giving away their now-obsolete 'high pitch' instruments. Arne B. rarely paid more than a couple of dollars for an instrument, if anything at all. He would then research its history, repair it, figure out how to play it, and place it on a shelf. He had become a collector.

During the Great Depression, with a "nickel in his pocket and cardboard in his shoes," Arne B. turned down the family occupation in farming and moved to the city. He studied at the Minneapolis College of Music and eventually earned a masters degree from Northwestern University in Evanston, Illinois. For several years, he taught public-school band in Minnesota. In 1943 he was hired to direct band and orchestra for the Brookings Public Schools. He moved his wife—a piano teacher herself—Jeanne Frances Kay Larson (1920–1986) and their son to South Dakota. His first child, André P. Larson (1942–2017), would grow up steeped in music and his father's instrument collection.

World War II's end brought more collecting opportunities. People in Great Britain eagerly traded musical instruments for tea, Spam, and other rationed goods. Arne B. also placed classified ads across the U.S.—always on the hunt for new and unusual instruments. All of Arne B.'s earnings from his weekend piano-tuning work went into growing the collection. By 1964, the Larson home was filled to capacity with more than 2,000 musical instruments. At the age of 60, Arne B. began looking for institutions that might be interested in the eclectic collection.

By collecting musical instruments, Arne Larson could collect their sounds.

Larson dreamed that someday a "Shrine of Music" might be created in southeastern South Dakota that would parallel in cultural magnitude the "Shrine of Democracy"—Mt. Rushmore—in western South Dakota.

Why is the National Music Museum in Vermillion, South Dakota?

The University of South Dakota recognized the educational potential of Arne B. Larson's instrument collection. Usher Abell (1915–2003), Chairman of the Department of Music, and Dr. Warren M. 'Doc' Lee (1908–1978), Dean of the College of Fine Arts, lobbied for the collection to come to USD. Commending Arne B.'s accomplishments also as a regionally respected music teacher and bandmaster, USD president I.D. Weeks (tenure of 1935 to 1966), offered him a position as professor of music. In the summer of 1966, a caravan of grain trucks rolled down the highway, each loaded with hundreds of Arne B.'s musical instruments, headed for their new home at USD in Vermillion.

When the I.D. Weeks Library opened at USD in 1967, the university's grand former Carnegie Library building was transformed for a new purpose—to house the Arne B. Larson Collection, the W. H. Over Museum, and the studio-gallery of famed Native-American painter Oscar Howe. By the 1990's the growing musical instrument collection occupied the entire Carnegie building.

A 'Shrine to Music'

Arne B. Larson was a collector, not an administrator; yet, he dreamed that someday a "Shrine of Music" might be created in southeastern South Dakota that would parallel in cultural magnitude the "Shrine of Democracy"—Mt. Rushmore—in western South Dakota. His son **André P. Larson** not only realized that dream of establishing a major musical-instrument museum on the Great Plains, he elevated its collections to world-class distinction.

Music was André P. Larson's birthright. Like his father, he began by playing clarinet at a young age. In the early 1960's, at the University of South Dakota, he pursued a B.F.A. in music education and a masters in music literature. His thesis topic? The double-reed instruments in his father's collection. For a few years André also owned and operated a music store in Brookings. Ultimately, he undertook doctoral studies at West Virginia University, finishing with a Ph.D. in musicology (his dissertation again focusing on instruments from his father's collection, this time, 19th-century British keyed brass).

Arne B. Larson was featured in two episodes about music and musical instruments on PBS's *Mr. Rogers' Neighborhood*, taped in Pittsburgh in 1973.

Through the efforts of Dr. Wayne S. Knutson (1926–2015), new Dean of the College of Fine Arts, and Martin Busch (1922–2011), founder of the South Dakota Public Broadcasting system, André was hired in 1972 to administer and develop his father's collection in Vermillion. In 1973, funded in part by the South Dakota Arts Council and the National Endowment for the Arts, André was appointed as the first director of the *Shrine to Music Museum* (renamed the *National Music Museum* in 2002). The musical instrument museum was born. A partnership of the University of South Dakota and a private board of trustees, the NMM is a public, non-profit, 501(c)(3) corporation.

André Larson focused on the development of the museum's collections—in his words, "*the ultimate measure of a museum's greatness*." The first three galleries opened in 1975, with Governor Richard F. Kneip present for ribbon cutting.

In 1979, Arne B. and Jeanne Larson officially donated their foundational collection of more than 2,500 instruments to the State of South Dakota. At that time, it was the largest single gift ever made to the University of South Dakota and also the largest single gift ever made in support of the arts in the state of South Dakota. Governor William Janklow presided over the ceremonies. Arne B. was also honored that year with the prestigious Governor's Award for Outstanding Support of the Arts and was elected to the South Dakota Hall of Fame. With his son André at the helm of the NMM, Arne B. continued on as the founder of the museum and its honorary first curator, never missing an opportunity to collect, until just a few years before his death in 1988.

André Larson went on to build yet more boldly on the original Larson holdings, inspiring benefactors to become passionate about the museum's mission. USD president Dr. Joseph 'Tip' McFadden (tenure 1982–1988) was an important champion. André elicited support for gallery development from trustees and friends including Barnes, Usher and Dr. Tom Abell; Dr. Grace Beede; Richard and Sharon Cutler; Margaret Ann and Hubert H. Everist; LaVonne and Clifford Graese; Mildred Lewison; Tom and Dr. Cindy Lillibridge; Friends of Senator Larry Pressler; and Bob and Marge Rawlins.

André P. Larson admires a bass lute by Andrea Harton, Venice, ca. 1600, one of the many treasures in the Witten-Rawlins Collection, 1984

This extraordinary donor generosity, as well as the proceeds from the 1983 sale of the Larson family farm in Minnesota, enabled André to "fill in the gaps" in the collection during the 1980s and through the early 2000s by acquiring many of the NMM's finest instruments. His goal was to create the preeminent institution of its kind in the world.

The NMM's collections now include many of the earliest, best-preserved, and

The NMM's collections now include many of the earliest, best preserved, and historically most important instruments known to survive.

historically most important instruments known to survive. Among André's favorites—acquired under his leadership and fundraising drive—are the famed "King" cello by Andrea Amati [p. 44], the "Harrison" Stradivari violin [p. 55], the 'Neapolitan' harpsichord [pp. 74–75], Johnny Cash and June Carter Cash's guitars [pp. 68–69], and the D'Angelico/D'Aquisto/Gudelsky guitar-workshop collection [p. 65].

André was also a professor of music at the University of South Dakota, where he established the nation's only graduate degree in the history of musical instruments. He was President of the American Musical Instrument Society (AMIS) from 1981–87 and was awarded the highest honor in his field, the AMIS Curt Sachs Award in 1990. He was elected to the South Dakota Hall of Fame in 2006. Finally, after 38 years of serving as the NMM's Founding Director, André

André P. Larson, flanked by mentor and NMM champion Dr. Wayne S. Knutson, enjoys his retirement celebration in 2011.

Larson retired in 2011. He passed away in 2017.
The museum's legacy as a world-class musical instrument collection, established by Arne B. and André P. Larson, has been carried on by several transitional leaders and directors, including Dr. Margaret Downie Banks, Ted Muenster, Dr. Cleveland Johnson, and Dr. Larry Schou. Through their combined efforts, as well as the passion and dedication of the Board of Trustees, museum staff, and USD president James Abbott (tenure 1997–2018), the NMM continues to thrive.

"Great Places, Great Faces"—A South Dakota motto

Many people have shared the NMM founders' passion for the establishment of an international institution on America's Great Plains. It is because of their ongoing generosity—providing their time, talents, non-cash gifts, and financial support—that the National Music Museum continues to flourish. A history of their giving deserves a book of its own. Here we can highlight only a few of the collections they made possible:

The Witten-Rawlins Collection

In 1984, the famed Witten Collection became available and the NMM was poised to acquire it. Laurence Witten had amassed an astounding collection of 16th to 19th-century Italian instruments and bows, including many of the earliest and historically most important stringed instruments known to survive. Included in this remarkable collection was a trio of unaltered and virtually new 18th-century instruments; two of only three classic Cremonese instruments that survive in nearly original, unaltered condition—the 1613 Brothers' Amati violino piccolo [p. 47] and the 1664 Andrea Guarneri tenor viola—as well as what is now thought of as the 'Mona Lisa' of the National Music Museum's collection, the incomparable Andrea Amati 'King' cello [p. 44]. The Witten Collection also included more than 65 violins, violas, cellos, lutes, guitars, and other instruments by the great 16th-, 17th-, and 18th-century masters, including work by three generations of the Amati family, plus 25 bows. Witten had also gathered original luthier tools, labels, and documentary materials, including important 16th-century books and prints.

Recognizing a once-in-a-lifetime opportunity to secure the museum's identity as a major cultural institution by acquiring the Witten collection, Director André P. Larson approached former USD graduates and museum patrons Robert (Bob) Ernest Rawlins (1911–1993) and Marjorie (Marge) Townsley Rawlins (1920–2009) for financial support. Without hesitation, the couple agreed to provide the millions of dollars needed to bid on the collection. In a high-profile competition with top American, German and Italian museums, the then-Shrine to Music Museum [now NMM] won. According to music critic Tim Page, in a 1984 Sunday *New York Times* article, the purchase was "believed to represent the largest sum ever paid by a museum for a collection of antique musical instruments."

Bob Rawlins (seated) and Marge Rawlins cutting the ribbon at Rawlins Gallery opening, NMM, 1986.

Bob and Marge Rawlins' generosity did not stop there. Their further funding made possible the purchase of the famed 'Harrison' Stradivari violin [p. 55] and the exceedingly rare Stradivari guitar now aptly known as the 'Rawlins' [p. 56]. The Rawlins gallery, where these instruments reside at the NMM, also bears the couple's name.

The Joe R. and Joella F. Utley Collection

The Joe R. & Joella F. Utley Collection of more than 600 brass instruments, donated to the National Music Museum in 1999, is a world-reknowned selection of cornets, trumpets, and related brass instruments amassed by Dr. Joe Utley (1935–2001) and his wife Joella. The Utley Collection is rich in European instruments from the 17th, 18th, and 19th centuries. An ornately decorated cornetto from the Rothschild Collection in Vienna [p. 23] is a masterpiece in ivory. The great brass makers of the Imperial City of Nürnberg—such as master Johann Wilhelm Haas [pp. 24 and 26]—are represented by half a dozen instruments. The inventor of the saxophone, Adolphe Sax, is represented by several stunning and historic instruments [pp. 34 and 35]. Filling what had been a major gap in the NMM's holdings, the Utleys also documented the work of many great 20th-century American trumpet makers.

The Alan G. Bates Collection

Alan Bates realized that harmonicas are not only small musical wonders but also special documents of cultural history. He resolved to build the best harmonica collection in this country. By about 1997, he had amassed 2,500 diverse models, including many of the finest, rarest and most novel [pp. 38–39], and had begun to search for the right museum in which to preserve them. In April of 2000, Bates' harmonica collection made the trek from Delaware to its new permanent home in Vermillion, South Dakota. The NMM's overall harmonica holdings are among the best in the world.

Percussion

INSTRUMENTS

A mallet strikes a *saron barung* of the NMM's Javanese gamelan. See pp. 20–21

King George I bass long drum

Maker unknown
England, between 1714 and 1727

One of the oldest known bass long drums.

The initials *G* and *R* spelled out in brass tacks on this early 18th-century bass drum stand for the Latin *George Rex*, referring to King George the 1st of England. The drum dates from the years of his reign and would have been played in a royal military band. The 2½-foot-long drum was worn strapped across the chest. The drummer would have played the strong beats with a wooden beater in one hand; the unstressed beats with a small stick in the other. The drum is made from one piece of mature elm, a wood more common to large-scale projects like shipbuilding than musical-instrument making.

NMM 10467
Board of Trustees, 2003

Snare (side) drum

William Kilbourn
Albany, New York, ca. 1861

Young Daniel "Stright" Bailey (1848–1932) stares out at us from a tintype photograph [seen atop the drum here]. He was only 12 when he and his brother served as members of the Fife and Drum Corps of Marshall County, Indiana, rallying troops for the Union's war effort. He was a drummer boy; his brother played fife. Daniel carried at his side this plain but sturdy snare.

In the Civil War era, craftsman William Kilbourn provided the military with snare drums, bass drums, tambourines, and banjos. One military contract, dated April 29, 1864, records Kilbourn being commissioned to produce 100 infantry drums for the Union army. Two Kilbourn drums, bearing makers labels, are in the NMM's collection. This snare is 14 inches tall by 16 inches in diameter. Basic and practical, it lacks the painted decoration or tack design characteristic of rope-tension military drums of this period.

The NMM boasts one of the finest public collections of Civil War musical instruments.

NMM 14910
Arne B. Larson Fund, 2014

Bowl gong (*kin*)

Maker unknown
Japan, ca. 1870

This imposing Japanese bowl gong and its opulent red-lacquered wooden stand are together more than four feet tall.

Painstakingly hand-hammered out of bronze, the thick-walled bowl has an almost iridescent patina.

At almost two feet across its upper end, the gong is cradled like a very large tea cup, atop a cushion placed on a heavy wood base.

The *kin* is associated with Buddhism, whether in religious ceremonies or in the sound effects and off-stage music of temple scenes in *kabuki* theater.

When played, the gong is struck on the rim in an upward movement with a large, leather-covered wooden mallet. The other-worldly deep echoing sound is remarkably powerful and long lasting and evokes a spiritual setting.

NMM 5561
Purchase funds gift of Margaret Ann and Hubert H. Everist, 1993

Thai goblet drum (*klong ae*)

Maker unknown
Thailand (Siam), late 19th century

No, it's not a cannon—though at ten feet long and weighing more than half a ton, this giant ceremonial drum is one of the largest instruments on display at the NMM. It is even transported on its own two-wheeled cart.

The goblet-shaped drum is carved from a single hollowed-out piece of *padauk* wood, covered with a cowhide drumhead.

Made in northern Siam in the late 19th century, large goblet drums were used in Buddhist temples to signal and regulate sacred activities. They were highly respected and never stepped over or touched with one's feet. They would also have been played in festive processions and to accompany folk dancing.

NMM 5405
Purchase funds gift of Clifford and LaVonne Graese, 1992

Goblet drum (*zarb* or *dombak*)

Maker unknown
Iran (Persia), ca. 1925

This *zarb* (or 'goblet' drum, so named for its drinking-glass shape) recalls the artistry of Persia and particularly, the Safavid style. The Safavid empire (1500–1722) was known for its artistic accomplishments and love of lyrical imagery.

This decorative drum is as much artist's canvas as musical instrument. Painted over a dark brown background, its flower-framed scenes depict women and men accompanied by sensory delights—food, wine, nature, conversation, and music. In one scene, a musician entertains two women on his *tār* (a Persian lute). The nightingale and the rose—a favorite Safavid symbol of love's longing—appears several times on this drum.

Zarbs of Persian classical music are usually made of wood and are not decorated with paintings. This elaborately painted example is made of clay with a goat-skin head—likely intended for the early 20th-century tourist trade rather than to be sold as a playable instrument.

NMM 2424
Purchase funds gift of Barnes and Usher Abell, 1978

Thumb piano (*sansa, mbira*)

Gbaya Tribe
Central Africa, ca. 1950

Sansas are often informally described as 'thumb pianos' because the tongues (lamellae) on the soundbox are plucked with the fingers to create musical sounds. (By contrast, the little metal lamellae in music boxes are also plucked—but by mechanical means.)

This elaborately carved Gbaya *sansa* is both a musical instrument and an evocative sculpture—representing a wide-eyed female figure with her hair pulled back. She is made from a hollowed-out block of wood and stands 19 inches tall.

Popular throughout sub-Saharan Africa, and also known also as *malimba*, *kisanji*, and by other names, thumb pianos may be played for personal enjoyment or to accompany singing during community gatherings.

NMM 4173
Gift of Verna Syverson, 1987

Gamelan

Ud Soepoyo
Surakarta, Java, Indonesia, 1999–2000

Originating in Indonesia centuries ago and varying by region, *gamelan* refers to a revered set of instruments, crafted and tuned to be played together: bronze gongs and pots, xylophone-like instruments with metal or wood bars, and drums. Gamelan also frequently include flutes, zithers, and spike fiddles. Using one of two tuning systems, *pélog* ('seven-note') or *slendro* ('five-note'), the instruments create intricate music.

The National Music Museum's Javanese gamelan is one of the largest and finest outside of Indonesia. Commissioned from Javanese master craftsman Ud Soepoyo, it was ceremoniously named *Kyai Rengga Manis Everist Gamelan* to honor its spiritual qualities and patronage. Radiant with gilding, its teakwood frames are adorned with carved dragons (*nagas*) and other lavish designs.

Gamelan are played to celebrate official events as well as individual and community milestones. The NMM's *Kyai Rengga Manis Everist Gamelan* comprises almost 70 instruments, many of which are regularly played at the NMM.

NMM 9857-9926
Commissioned, 1999
Purchase funds gift of Margaret Ann Everist

Wind
INSTRUMENTS

Holton Sousaphone, 1926, p. 37

Ivory cornetto (*Zink*)

Maker unknown
Southern Germany, ca. 1600

In 1938, Nazi SS agents confiscated this cornetto and other masterpieces from the famed Rothschild family in Vienna, Austria. Decades later, unlike countless objects plundered from other Jewish collectors throughout the Holocaust, this cornetto was returned to descendants of the original owners. The Rothschild family then offered the cornetto at a famous Christie's London auction in 1999. The National Music Museum acquired "The Rothschild" at that time.

This rare cornetto was fashioned from a single elephant tusk. Eight smooth sides were carved along its curved length. Tracings of gold still enhance the black designs engraved into the ivory.

A Renaissance relative of the trumpet, the cornetto produces a soft, high-pitched sound, likened to the human voice, and was often used to accompany choirs.

NMM 7368
Joe R. and Joella F. Utley Collection, 1999

Miniature natural horn

Johann Wilhelm Haas (1649–1723)
Nuremberg, 1681

This exquisite horn is the earliest work in existence by master maker Johann Wilhelm Haas. It was crafted in the year Haas's youngest son, Wolf Wilhelm (1681–1760), was born and may have been made to commemorate his birth or baptism. (Wolf would eventually take over his father's workshop.) And yet, the presence of a city of Nuremberg quality-inspection mark on the horn would have also made it suitable for purchase.

Although very small, this single-coil horn can produce two notes an octave apart. Typically, octave leaps were sounded by riders to signal the arrival of the mail. Miniature horns made of precious metals were sometimes used as status symbols by postal officials of the time.

Elaborately decorated, the horn is solid silver with gold-plating inside the bell and on the mouthpiece.

Four angel heads surround the gilded bell garland, around which is also engraved the date and maker's name, as well as his unique maker's mark—a leaping hare. Haas means "hare" in German.

NMM 7213
Joe R. and Joella F. Utley Collection, 1999

Alto recorder

Johann Benedikt Gahn (1674–1711)
Nuremberg, ca. 1698–1711

This fancifully carved creature with human-like eyes is actually an alto recorder—the handiwork of master wood-turner and musical-instrument maker Johann Benedikt Gahn.

One of only 14 known existing altos by Gahn, this 19-inch-long instrument also features the ornate acanthus-leaf designs and patterns so typical of his style and of other Nuremberg makers of the time.

Gahn, who worked often with ivory, made this recorder from European boxwood, another classic material for woodwind instruments of the Renaissance and Baroque periods. Boxwood is a very dense, hard wood with a fine grain and silky surface, ideal for holding crisp carved detail. A trace of a maker's mark is still identifiable on the body.

The sweet-sounding alto became the preferred recorder size around 1700. It predominates in both chamber and orchestral music.

NMM 4142
Rawlins Fund, 1987

Natural trumpet

Johann Wilhelm Haas (1649–1723)
Nuremberg, ca. 1720

Imagine a royal celebration of centuries past, trumpets blazing. A natural trumpet—like this one—might have played those fanfares. This Haas natural trumpet is believed to have heralded the wedding of a countess in 1720. It is made of expensive materials, solid silver with gold-plating, and is adorned with military figures, trumpets, and drums.

For rulers in Europe, Haas was the go-to trumpet workshop. Founded by Johann Wilhelm Haas in 1676, it existed for more than four generations in Nuremberg. Haas family craftsmen signed their instruments with the founder's initials *IWH* and master's mark—the hare. But the hare's pose—looking forward *or* reverently back at the founder's initials—hints at which dynasty member crafted the instrument.

Yet, this trumpet presents an enigma: The city inspection mark on its bell garland is from the time of Johann Wilhelm Haas. But the engraved date 1765 suggests that the trumpet was made by his grandson Ernst Johann Conrad Haas. Research on the markings has led to the hypothesis that the 1765 date was added later, possibly by the countess's heirs.

NMM 5071
Arne B. and Jeanne F. Larson Fund; funds given in memory of Grace L. Beede by Helen and Robert D. Thorne; and funds gift of Clifford and LaVonne Graese, 1991

Oboe

Hendrik Richters (1683–1727)
Amsterdam, ca. 1720

By the late 1600's, the versatile and expressive tone of the oboe gave it a predominant role in the woodwind section of orchestras. Oboes made by the Dutch brothers Hendrik and Fredrik Richters were not only among the finest of these musical instruments, but works of art as well.

Reflecting Richters' style, each of this oboe's three silver keys is engraved with tiny images, symbols and scenes. On the C key, a visual puzzle (rebus) of an etched barrel, winged hourglass, ladder, and globe is thought to translate into a very Enlightenment-minded meme: *Grasp time and learn to know the world.*

This oboe's three sections are made of finely turned ebony wood. The top mount and trim are made of exquisitely lathed ivory—in precise patterns resembling basketwork and reeds.

H. RICHTERS is stamped on all three of the oboe's joints.

NMM 4547
Arne B. and Jeanne F. Larson Fund, 1989

Clarinet in A

August Grenser (1720–1807)
Dresden, 1785

The oldest clarinet at the National Music Museum is also the earliest known clarinet in A by renowned woodwind-master August Grenser.

It is also one of only a few surviving clarinets by this esteemed maker.

Official maker to the prince-elector of Saxony, Grenser created instruments that were prized for their exceptional tone and intonation.

Superbly crafted of boxwood, with brass keys, this clarinet has four sections. Letters and numbers on the sections suggest the clarinet had additional interchangeable parts, which would have allowed it to be played in either A *or* B-flat pitches. But only the A sections remain.

This Grenser also originally had only four keys, typical of early clarinets, which were just becoming mainstream instruments. The fifth key was probably added later on, to help make the fingering easier. The five-key form became the standard throughout most of the first half of the nineteenth century.

NMM 7385
Purchase funds gift of Tom and Cindy Lillibridge, 1999

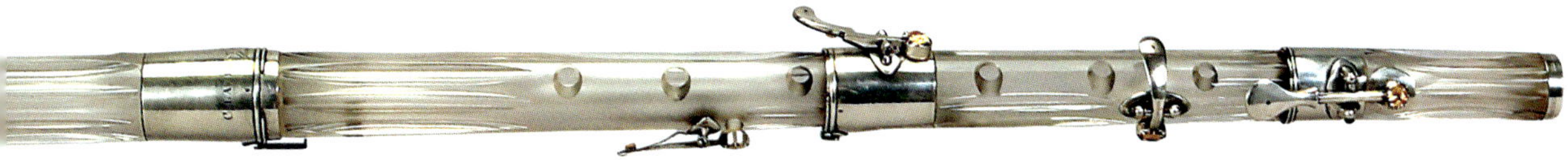

Glass flute

Claude Laurent (1774–1849)
Paris, ca. 1817

As status symbols in the age of industrial progress and empire, Claude Laurent's elegant cut-glass flutes were often gifts to heads of state. Emperor Napoleon I and U.S. President James Madison were both Laurent owners.

Parisian clockmaker Laurent patented his 'crystal flute' in 1806, winning a silver medal for his invention that year at the Paris Industrial Exposition. Laurent believed that glass resisted humidity (including the breath of flutists) and was more stable than wood and ivory. Scientific research has since shown that many of Laurent's flutes were made not of leaded crystal but of potash glass, which, ironically, *is* susceptible to humidity, resulting over time in flaking and microscopic cracking that creates a frosted look.

The cap at the end of this flute is diamond-cut glass. The keys are embellished with small gemstones. Engraved on the silver ferrule at the flute's head joint is the makers' signature and patent claim: *C. LAURENT À PARIS / Breveté*.

NMM 10103
Purchase funds gift of Tom and Cindy Lillibridge, 2001

Serpent

Makers unknown
England,
Copper, ca. 1825–1830
Melton, ca. 1810–1820

Serpent—of course!—is the name of these snake-shaped wind instruments. Most were made of two hollowed-out halves of leather-covered wood. More than two feet long, they are usually played vertically.

From the 1700s until the early 1900s, serpents were used in French churches to accompany singing. In the early 1800s, serpents became popular in English village and military bands.

The royal coat of arms of England with lion and unicorn is painted in gold on this Melton serpent. The inscription *MELTO[N] BAND* tells us the instrument belonged to the Melton village band, Leicestershire.

In rainy England, serpents were often made out of metal for outdoor use and for military bands. This thick copper example has brass trimmings.

Wood and copper serpents sound remarkably similar—deep and round—because the shape of the tubing inside them, more than their material, determines the character of their sound.

Awkward to hold and difficult to play in tune, serpents were eventually surpassed by tubas and other brass instruments.

Copper serpent, NMM 2677
Board of Trustees, 1980

Melton serpent, NMM 1279
Arne B. Larson Collection, 1979

Bassoon

Jean Nicolas Savary the Younger (1786–1853)
Paris, 1823

This may have been both the prototype and the only bassoon of its kind built by renowned French maker Jean Nicolas Savary. Many of his instruments survive, but this appears to be the sole example of a model known otherwise only from 1823 advertisements.

Savary was the leading bassoon maker in Paris in the early 1800's, a time of cutting-edge technological experimentation. This particular bassoon features innovative mechanically operated tuning slides.

Since pitch was not standardized at this time, instruments that could easily be tuned no matter the pitch promised to be more versatile.

Why didn't this prototype become a product? With its 'high-tech' mechanisms, elegant tiger-maple body, and octagonal mahogany case, the bassoon may have just been too expensive to reproduce, dooming it to commercial failure.

NMM 2418
Ringley Fund, 1978

Tortoise-shell keyed bugle

George W. Shaw (1807–1875)
Thompson, Connecticut, ca. 1845

Only two tortoise-shell keyed bugles made by George W. Shaw survive: one at the Smithsonian in Washington, D.C., and this one at the NMM, a piccolo (about 9 1/2 inches high), which is smaller than any other known keyed bugle.

Tortoise shell—the actual shell of the animal—was once used as we use plastic today and is found in furniture inlay and on luxury items such as combs and snuffboxes.

On musical instruments, tortoise shell was a popular material for covering keys, decorating bowed and plucked stringed instruments, and even encasing the body of a wooden flute or recorder. But it was rarely used as a structural element.

Shaw was so fascinated by the material that he applied in 1845 for a U.S. patent for keyed bugles made entirely of tortoise shell. Quite fragile and lacking the warm, full sound of a normal metal keyed bugle, Shaw's version never caught on.

NMM 7070
Joe R. and Joella F. Utley Collection, 1999

Bagpipe (*dudy, bock*)

Maker unknown
Bohemia, ca. 1850

Bagpipes aren't just from Scotland. Variations are found in many countries and reach back into antiquity. This *dudy* or *bock*—meaning 'billy goat'—bagpipe came from southwestern Bohemia (modern-day Czech Republic), but similar ones are also found throughout Eastern Europe as well as in Southern Germany and Austria.

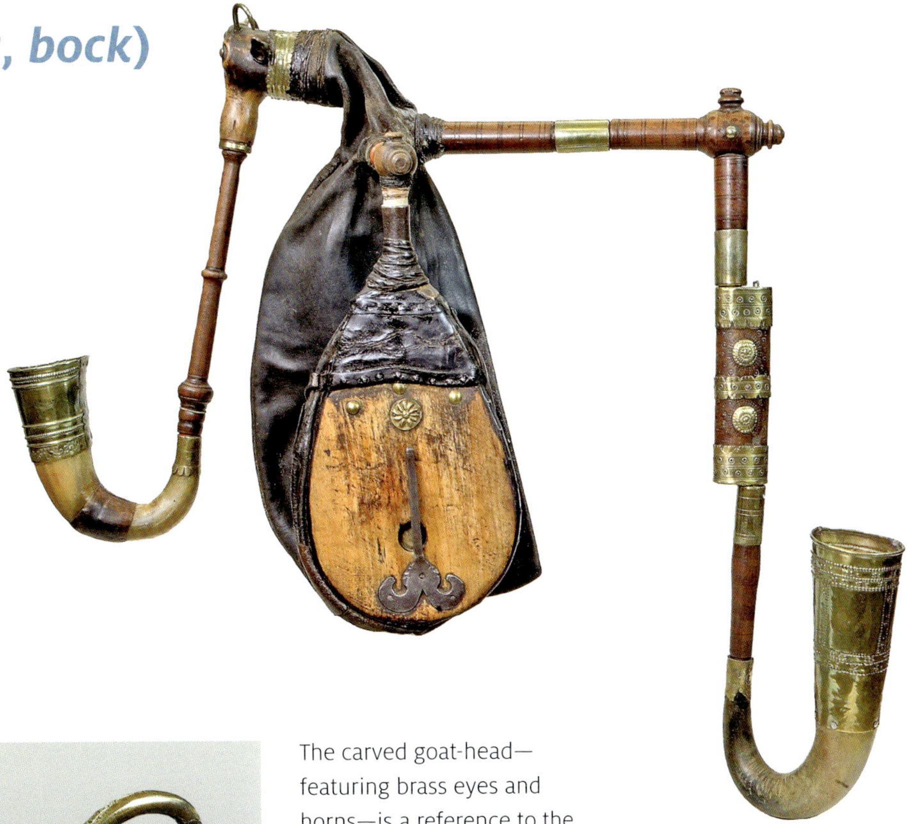

The carved goat-head—featuring brass eyes and horns—is a reference to the traditional use of goatskin for the instrument's bag or body.

Both the chanter, on which the melody is played, and the drone pipe are decorated with engraved brass work over cow-horn bells.

This type of bagpipe is not inflated by the player's breath but by bellows pumped under the arm, allowing the piper to sing while playing. The drone pipe, which sounds one constant pitch, is carried over the player's right shoulder.

NMM 1270
Arne B. Larson Collection, 1979

Tenor saxophone in B-flat

Adolphe Sax (1814–1894)
Paris, ca. 1861

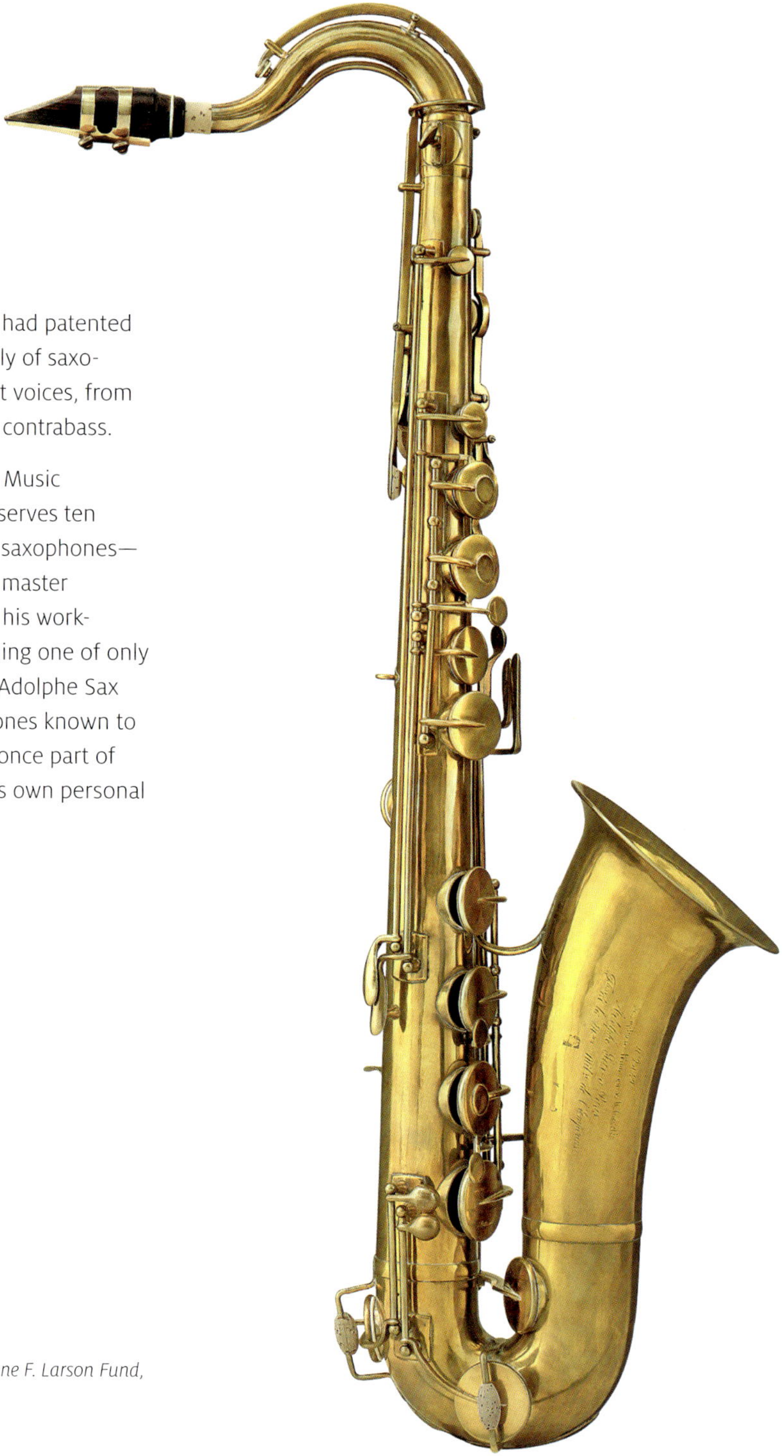

Belgian inventor and musical genius Adolphe Sax combined the best of the woodwinds and brasses to create what had never been heard before: the saxophone. The instrument would go well beyond its original commission in 19th-century French army bands—taking on a life never imagined by Sax. And yet, the contemporary saxophone—of jazz, pop, classical music and more—has not changed dramatically since Sax's brilliant original.

Engraved with serial number, maker's name, and monogram, this tenor saxophone's delicate brass body is much lighter than that of modern instruments. And with its shorter bell, this sax cannot go as low as today's saxes.

By 1846, Sax had patented a whole family of saxophones, eight voices, from sopranino to contrabass.

The National Music Museum preserves ten Adolphe Sax saxophones—made by the master himself or in his workshop—including one of only a handful of Adolphe Sax bass saxophones known to survive, and once part of the inventor's own personal collection.

NMM 4039
Arne B. and Jeanne F. Larson Fund, 1986

6-valve trombone in B-flat

Adolphe Sax (1814–1894)
Paris, 1887

Adolphe Sax's greatest legacy was the saxophone, but he made many other innovative—if not as wildly successful—instruments.

Seeking to make a better trombone, Sax created this trombone in B-flat with six independent piston valves for superior tuning. Great in theory, less so in practice: the more intricate metalwork was costly to manufacture (and purchase), weighed the instrument down, and was more complicated to play. Few were made.

Sax's bold lifework typifies the spirit and advances of the Industrial Revolution, with his experimentation in metalworking, valve technologies, and production methods. The National Music Museum preserves many other Sax masterworks: his popular saxhorns, the short-lived saxotromba, his soprano ophicleide, a grand-parade trumpet, and a 6-valve trumpet in F.

The NMM also owns instruments by Adolphe Sax's father, Charles-Joseph, and son, Adolphe-Edouard. The Sax family dynasty reigned in the Brussels and Paris markets from the early 1800's to early 1900's, making vital contributions to the evolution of music.

NMM 4656
Arne B. and Jeanne F. Larson Fund, 1986

Buffalo horn (*ngeku*)

Maker unknown
Nepal, ca. 1900–1925

This elaborate Tibetan horn is made from a hollow water buffalo horn, encircled with highly decorated copper and silver cuffs and other fittings. Near the bell of this 18-inch horn is the forbidding bronze head of a mythical sea-dragon, studded with turquoise stone eyes. This water monster (*makara)* is a symbol of strength and defiance, designed to scare away evil spirits, especially any attracted to the horn's music.

Further spiritual favor comes from the Eight Auspicious Symbols that are etched into the metal work. These Tibetan Buddhist decorative motifs represent a host of attributes—from abundance and purity, valor and victory, wisdom and compassion, to the overcoming of suffering and adversity.

Traditionally played by members of the Nepali musician caste to entertain aristocratic Buddhists living in Nepal, *ngeku* horns are now played by street performers and in local festivals.

NMM 2352
Purchase funds gift of Mrs. Clark Y. (Ethel) Gunderson, 1977

Sousaphone in BB-flat

Holtonphone Mammoth Model 130
Frank Holton & Co., Elkhorn, Wisconsin, 1926

The press at a 1927 music tradeshow in Iowa raved: This "bass horn [sousaphone] is said to have cost $2,000 alone to build and contains $800 worth of gold. The engraver worked four months on the elaborate decorations of the bell, which is a work of art itself."

This extraordinary sousaphone represented Holton-brand brass instruments at exhibitions in the 1920's and 30's and ultimately graced the main office of the Wisconsin firm until its closure in 2008. It was a fitting symbol: Company founder Frank Holton had been a principal musician in John Philip Sousa's famed band. Named for the renowned bandmaster, a sousaphone is a type of large-belled tuba that wraps around the player's body.

Measuring 29 inches across, the gold-plated bell of this sousaphone is covered with handcrafted cast-bronze medallions, including lyres, horns, ribbons, and an elk head symbolizing Elkhorn, Holton's Wisconsin headquarters.

NMM 13798
Gift of Conn-Selmer, Inc., 2008

Harmonicas

The NMM has one of the most outstanding public harmonica collections in the world.

Many of the 2,500+ harmonicas in the NMM's Bates Collection—donated by expert Alan G. Bates—are among the finest anywhere.

Academically categorized as 'Western mouth organs' and informally called "harps" by many fans, harmonicas are fairly recent musical instruments, dating from the early 1800's. Mass production has made them accessible to amateur and professional players of all ages. Easy to learn (harder to master), the harmonica is an instrument for the people. Its many forms reflect its historical moments, popular culture, musicians' aspirations, and sometimes just pure gimmickry and fun.

Clockwise from top on this page:
Wheatstone Symphonium, 1829, NMM 10877; Wheatstone Triple Aeolina & case, ca. 1830, NMM 10434; Ivory harmonica, ca. 1873, NMM 14970.

Among the high notes of the NMM's Alan G. Bates collection:

A precursor to the harmonica, the tiny, rare **Symphonium**, was made in London, England, by Victorian inventor/scientist Charles Wheatstone in 1829. The player blows into the front hole and pushes buttons to obtain different notes.

Taking its name from the ancient Greek wind god, the rare, pocket-sized **Triple Æolina**, 1830, is another Wheatstone forerunner of the harmonica. Its three German-silver reed plates, framed in ivory, fit conveniently into a plush leather case. London, England.

One of the most valuable harmonicas at the NMM—this carved **ivory harmonica** (circa 1873) with gold-plated reed plates is one of only a few surviving by Viennese maker Georg Bruckbauer.

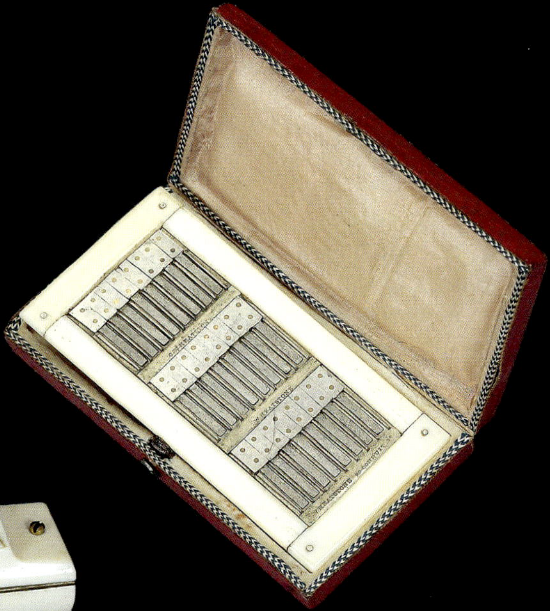

At just over an inch long, this **miniature, nine-carat gold-plated harmonica** is one of the smallest playable harmonicas. Maker unknown, ca. 1930.

The whimsical tin **"Gold-Fisch" harmonica** was introduced in 1905 by the Andreas Koch Company, Trossingen, Germany.

Among the most desired, for its novelty, the Hohner **"Trumpet Call" harmonica** features five purely decorative brass horns. Trossingen, Germany, 1923.

The 1924 **Zeppelin harmonica** was made by the German company C. A. Seydel Söhne to commemorate the airship *Los Angeles*, made in Germany for the U.S. Navy and first flown that year. Untersachsenberg-Georgenthal (Klingenthal), Germany.

Turn the handle on this M. Hohner **"Tremolo Sextet" paddle-wheel harmonica** to select one of the six built-in harmonicas tuned in six keys. Trossingen, Germany, ca. 1939.

CLOCKWISE FROM TOP ON THIS PAGE:
Miniature gold harmonica, ca. 1930, NMM 7509; Koch Goldfisch harmonica, 1905, NMM 9232; "Trumpet Call" harmonica, 1923, NMM 8293; Seydel-Söhne "Los Angeles" Zeppelin-harmonica, 1924, NMM 7735; Paddle-wheel harmonica, ca. 1939, NMM 9212

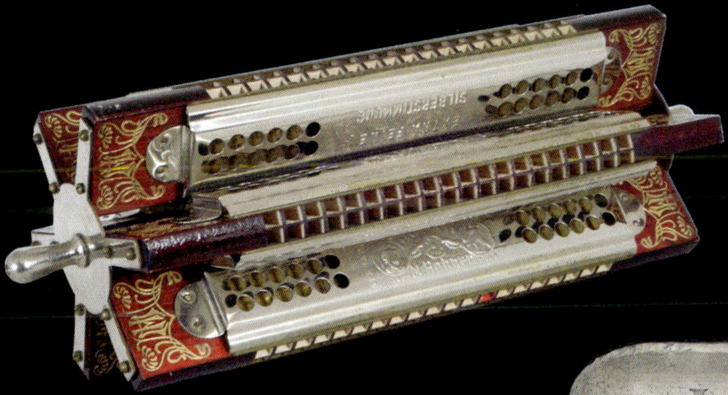

Jazzophone in B-flat

Possibly by Franz Xaver Hüller
(1856–1936)
Graslitz, Czechoslovakia,
ca. 1926–1935

A two-headed sax? A musical telephone? No, it's a Jazzophone—a quirky and novel instrument that had a short but promising run between the World Wars.

The wildfire spread of American jazz music in the 1920's, especially in Europe, put saxophonists and affordable saxophones in short demand. Enter the Jazzophone, in 1926, a less expensive instrument that was actually a two-belled trumpet with the curvy look of the saxophone. With its trumpet mouthpiece and valves (three regular, plus one to switch bells), the Jazzophone was marketed to trumpeters. It produced not only a trumpet sound on one bell but the popular jazzy 'wah-wah' sound on the other with its handy built-in mute.

Registered by Franz Xaver Hüller, the Jazzophone was produced by German and Czech firms. Ultimately, the Jazzophone may have been doomed by the rise of the anti-jazz Nazi Reich—or, less ominously—by the fact, that for all its charm, it was neither a full trumpet nor 'saxy' enough to replace a saxophone.

NMM 5445
Arne B. Larson Collection, 1979

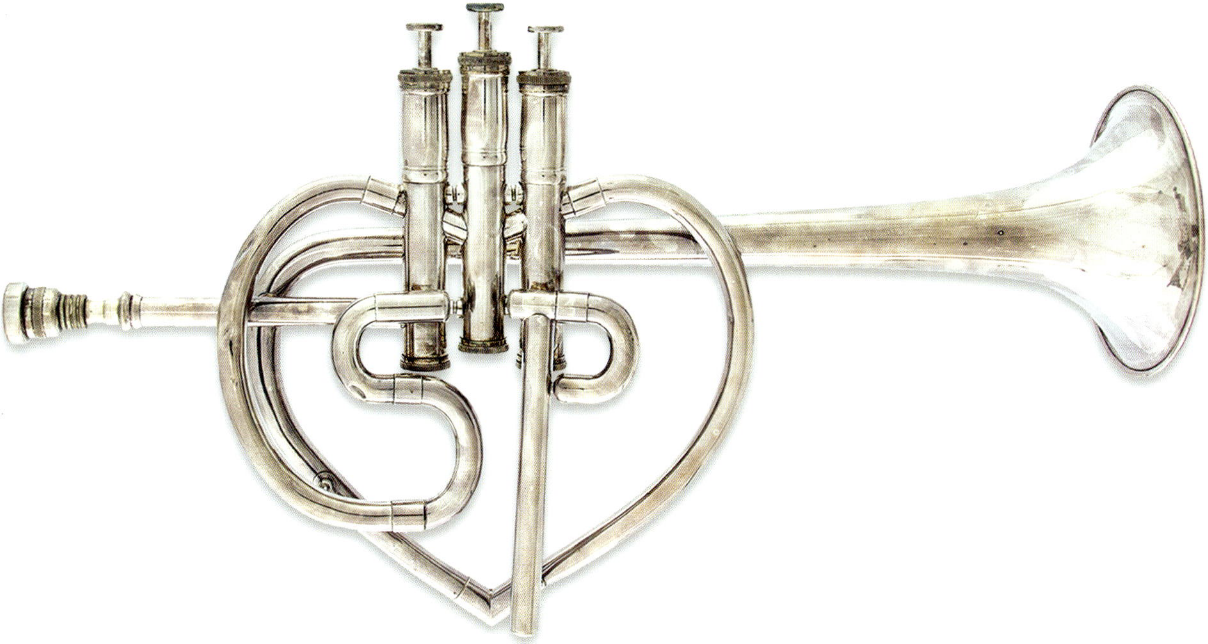

Sgt. Pepper trumpet

Dominick Calicchio (1901–1979)
Hollywood, California, 1978

"These instruments have the power to make dreams come true . . ."
— From the movie *Sgt. Pepper's Lonely Hearts Club Band*, 1978

This heart-shaped trumpet was built by master craftsman Dominick Calicchio of Hollywood as a central prop for the 1978 movie *Sgt. Pepper's Lonely Hearts Club Band*. The film featured music by the Beatles and an all-star cast that included the Bee Gees; Peter Frampton; George Burns; Aerosmith; Earth, Wind, and Fire; and a parade of other celebrities. Widely panned by critics, it was wildly embraced by fans later as a cult classic.

The silver-plated instrument steals many scenes, including the 'Maxwell Silver Hammer' number, featuring comedian Steve Martin, and the 'Get Back' number, with Billy Preston.

Calicchio masterfully captured the look of the 1970's in the turns of the trumpet's tubing: Sgt. Pepper's initials *S* and *P* are pure pop-art font.

This unplayable trumpet was one of only two made for the movie by Italian-immigrant maker Calicchio, who meticulously handcrafted some 2,000 *playable* brass instruments in his lifetime.

NMM 6176
Purchase funds gift of Allan R. Jones, in memory of Marjorie M. Jones, 1998

Clinton saxophone

"No. 1 Bill Clinton"
L.A. Sax Company
Barrington, Illinois, 1993

"That is the most beautiful saxophone I have ever seen," remarked President Bill Clinton, before playing a few favorite jazz riffs on it.

Number One of a limited edition of 150 *LA-42T Presidential Model* saxophones, this instrument was designed to honor President Bill Clinton. It was presented to him on May 16, 1994, by the CEO of the L.A. Sax Company during a ceremony in the Oval Office.

Clinton's 1992 campaign appearance playing sax on the *Arsenio Hall Show* was credited with causing sax sales in the U.S. to soar. After Clinton's presidential win, manufacturer L.A. Sax developed this commemorative-edition instrument.

The sax is finished in 'metallic fire red, diamond metallic white and reflex blue' lacquer with iconic stars covering the bell flare. Two gold-plated plaques document the Clinton provenance.

Presidents may not keep gifts, so Clinton presented the saxophone to the NMM at the Oval Office meeting, attended by Congressman Tim Johnson (of Vermillion), Senator Larry Pressler, and University of South Dakota Vice President John Hilpert.

NMM 5727
Gift of President William Jefferson Clinton, 1994

Stringed
INSTRUMENTS

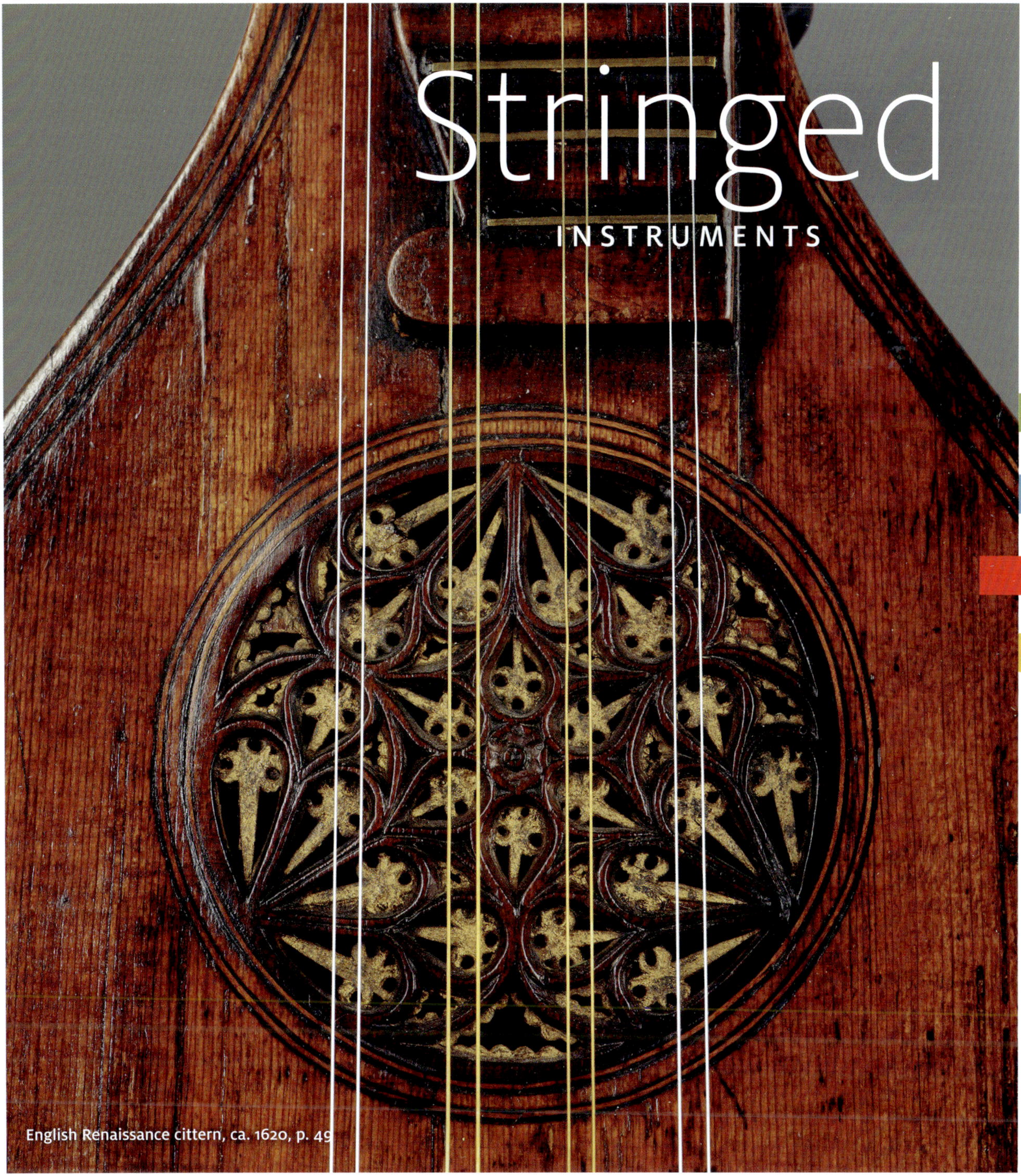

English Renaissance cittern, ca. 1620, p. 49

Amati 'King' cello

Andrea Amati (ca. 1505–1577)
Cremona, Italy, after 1538

The crown jewel of the National Music Museum.

Thought to be the *earliest surviving cello*, the 'King' is one of the most famous musical instruments in the world. It was made by Cremonese master Andrea Amati, founder of the most important violin-making tradition in history. His workshop trained or influenced future generations of Italian makers, including his sons, grandson, and Antonio Stradivari.

The Amati workshop made sets of instruments for the French Royal Court, beginning as early as 1536. Some of these, including the 'King,' may have been repurposed and repainted for later sets. The instrument's early features, including its upright soundholes, may pre-date the painted imagery done during King Charles IX's reign, 1560 to 1574.

Both a musical and artistic masterpiece, the 'King' cello is decorated with gilded symbols and images related to Charles IX. On the back, the female figure of "Justice" wields a sword, representing this monarchy's claim to divine justice. The Latin words for piety and justice, as well as the letter 'K' for *Karolus* (Charles) are painted on the cello's sides.

Typical of the finest Cremonese instruments, the front of the cello is made of fine Alpine spruce; the back of maple.

Remarkably, the 'King' still plays beautifully: its tones are deep and rich.

Originally a larger instrument (the bass violin of the Renaissance violin band), the 'King' was reduced in size and restored to playing condition at the beginning of the 19th century for use as a classical-period violoncello.

Passing through generations of royal and aristocratic hands to generations of citizen owners after the French Revolution and finally reigning now in the Witten-Rawlins Collection at the NMM, the 'King' cello is a stunning witness to more than 400 hundred years of musical and political history.

NMM 3351
Witten-Rawlins Collection, 1984

Amati viola

Andrea Amati (ca. 1505–1577)
Cremona, Italy, ca. 1559

More instrument royalty.

This viola is one of the best preserved of the surviving stringed instruments by Italian Renaissance maker Andrea Amati.

Emblems on the viola suggest it was made and painted for King Phillip II of Spain and Elisabeth of Valois, daughter of French king Henry II. Their 1559 power-marriage unified the Catholic royal courts of Hapsburg and Valois against the threats of Protestantism. The Latin motto in gold on the viola's back proclaims "By this one bulwark, religion stands and will stand."

NMM 3370
Witten-Rawlins Collection, 1984

'King Henry IV' violin

Antonio and Girolamo Amati
(1540–1638 and 1556–1630)
Cremona, Italy, ca. 1595

Fit for a king!

This Brothers Amati violin bears the emblems of King Henry IV (1553–1610), the last French ruler to order violins from the Amatis for the royal court. Painted in black and gold on the violin's maple ribs is the Latin for 'Henry IV, by the Grace of God, King of France and Navarre.'

The brothers Antonio and Girolamo Amati carried on the tradition of fine stringed-instrument making begun by their renowned father Andrea Amati. Like him, they were commissioned to make instruments for the French royal court. The NMM is the only institution to have examples from all four known sets of Amati instruments painted for the French court in the 16th century.

A 19th-century inscription on the inside of the instrument documents its further history, including ownership by the celebrity French violin soloist and teacher Jean-Baptiste Cartier.

The violin survives with an exquisite Louis XVI-era wood case covered in tooled leather, bearing the triple *fleur-de-lys* symbol of the French royal court.

The 'King Henry the IV' violin is one of the NMM's extraordinary collection of nine Amati-family instruments.

NMM 14470
Purchase funds gift of Kevin Schieffer, 2010

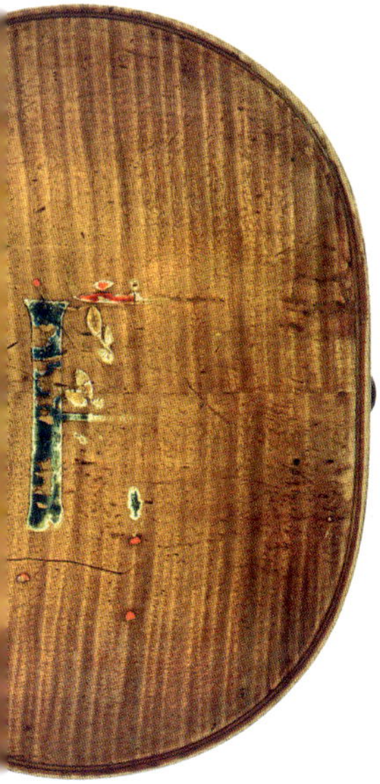

Violino piccolo

Girolamo Amati (1556–1630)
Cremona, Italy, 1613

One of the most intact Renaissance stringed instruments in existence—and *no, it's not a toy.*

This small-sized ('piccolo') violin by one of the famed Amati brothers is about 3/4 of the size of a modern standard violin and was designed for adults. Musicians could play the high passages in music without having to move their hand far up the fingerboard.

It is also a rare glimpse at what the finest Renaissance instruments looked like when they were made – preserved as it is, in perfect, original condition with a delicately inlaid maple fingerboard.

Most surviving 16th- and 17th-century Cremonese instruments were altered at some time to meet the changing needs of musicians and evolving concepts of the 'ideal sound.' (Sometimes necks and internal parts were replaced; sometimes different fingerboards and tailpieces were installed.) Perhaps because these very small, high-pitched violins eventually became obsolete, this little Amati was spared 'updating'—surviving more than 400 years unscathed.

NMM 3361
Witten-Rawlins Collection, 1984

Pamir rubab (long-necked lute)

Maker unknown
Pamir Mountains, Central Asia
ca. 1616–1617

Among the great historic instruments of the National Music Museum is this extraordinarily rare *rubab*—crafted some 400 years ago in the Pamir Mountains of central Asia. The east-west trade routes of the Silk Road were bustling. In Renaissance Europe, Shakespeare was living his last year, and young violinmaker Nicolò Amati was learning his family's famed art.

The NMM's *Pamir rubab* is the earliest-known surviving example of such an instrument, though stringed instruments of this name are mentioned as early as the 9th century. A Persian inscription on the back of the *rubab* translates as this: *"The dearest precious rubab, heritage/inheritance in the name of Seyyed Hasan Shah, the year 1025"* [this date, from the Islamic lunar Hijri calendar, correlates roughly to 1616–1617].

The sculptural body, long neck, and pegbox of this lute are made of one piece of fruitwood. The body is covered with leather, tacked with eight metal nails. At one time, this *rubab* had eight strings, though now it has just six.

NMM 5580
Board of Trustees, 1993

Cittern

Maker unknown
England, ca. 1620

This is the *only English Renaissance cittern known to survive*—despite the popularity of these instruments in the Elizabethan and Jacobean era.

English citterns were compact and portable, played in barber shops and other casual venues. Plucked with a pick, the eight metal strings made for a bright, twanging sound.

Carved above a cittern's pegs were grotesque or comical figures and faces—in this instance, the head of a howling dog. Shakespeare even used "cittern head" as an insult in his play *Love's Labor's Lost*!

The front of this cittern is made of spruce. The back is made of alternating strips of maple and plum, woods also found on historic viols of the same time period. The intricately carved wood and gilded-parchment soundhole is referred to as a 'rose.'

Like the NMM's ivory cornetto (p. 23), this cittern was once owned by famed collectors Nathaniel and Albert von Rothschild. In 2007, the NMM acquired it at auction.

NMM 13500
Arne B. and Jeanne F. Larson Fund, 2007

Nicolò Amati violin

Nicolò Amati (1596–1684)
Cremona, Italy, 1628

Nicolò Amati survived the bubonic plague.

So the violin did too.

In the epidemic that raged across Italy from 1629 to 1631, one out of three people perished. Among them, in Cremona, was Nicolò's master-maker father Girolamo, son of innovator Andrea Amati. In the rival violin-making town of Brescia, the plague struck down master-craftsman Giovanni Paolo Maggini.

It fell to Nicolò to carry on the tradition of the Amati workshop and the Cremonese school. He not only shared the craft outside of his family—he advanced it, with masterpieces of his own. Nicolò is now regarded the greatest maker of the Amati dynasty.

The tradition that Nicolò saved would profoundly influence the art of stringed-instrument making, engendering a 'greatest generation' of luthiers: Nicolò Amati himself, Andrea Guarneri (ca. 1626–1698), Austrian master Jacob Stainer (ca. 1619–1683), and the most famous of violinmakers, Antonio Stradivari (1644–1737).

A crown jewel of the NMM's collections, this pristine violin bears an authentic Antonio and Hieronymus (Girolamo) Amati label but was actually made by Nicolò.

Made of golden-varnished spruce and maple, the violin builds on the stellar workmanship and sound quality achieved by Nicolò's famed grandfather Andrea (maker of the NMM's famed Amati 'King' cello, p. 44). This brilliant instrument is still widely copied and reinterpreted by violinmakers.

NMM 3356
Witten-Rawlins Collection, 1984

Archlute

Pieter Railich (1615–ca. 1678)
for Matteo Sellas (ca. 1599–1654)

Ebony and ivory live together in perfect harmony. . . .

One of the most eye-catching objects at the National Music Museum is the black-and-white ribbed archlute by craftsman Pieter Railich. This was a status symbol and luxury item in its own time—not fashioned from ordinary wood as most lutes were. Strips of ebony and ivory, imported from as far away as Africa, adorn the back of this 28-string (14 double-course) Baroque instrument.

Like many lutemakers in Venice, Pieter (or, 'Pietro') Railich was probably originally from an instrument-making family in Bavaria but gravitated to Italy to work in one of its acclaimed instrument-making centers. Lutes were among the most popular of instruments and some of the first produced in great quantities.

For this particular archlute, Railich was 'subcontracted' to work for the famed stringed-instrument maker and dealer Matteo Sellas. A printed Sellas label is visible through the intricately hand-carved soundhole. However, Railich, the actual builder, cleverly concealed his own signature deep inside the instrument.

NMM 3383
Witten-Rawlins Collection, 1984

Stainer violin

Jacob Stainer (c. 1619–1683)
Absam bei Innsbruck, Austria, 1668

Before Stradivari, there was Stainer.

Considered by many to be the greatest violin-maker of the 17th century, Jacob Stainer has also been called the greatest outside of the Italian tradition. Today, violins of the Italian masters are preferred by soloists, but in the 17th and 18th century many violinists preferred the sweet, silvery tone of the Stainer model.

With the exception of its newer pegs and a little wear to the varnish, this Stainer violin is preserved in the same condition in which it left the maker's shop over 340 years ago. The neck is original and typical of those on 17th-century instruments: straight—not tilted back—as necks are on violins today. This violin is an excellent example of the highly arched yet elegant Stainer model that was widely imitated during his lifetime and after.

Not long after this violin was made, Stainer was denounced for religious heresy. The years of persecution to come affected not only his well-being but his productivity. Comparatively few of his stringed masterpieces exist. This particular violin may have survived because it was made for a convent and was literally cloistered for its first 250 years.

This violin and a rare Stainer tenor viola (circa 1650) are among the crown jewels of the National Music Museum.

NMM 4548
Board of Trustees, in memory of Arne B. and Jeanne F. Larson, 1988

The Antonio Stradivari collection

The National Music Museum preserves one of the finest collections of stringed instruments by Antonio Stradivari (1644–1737)—not only the great 'Harrison' violin but also a guitar, a viola da gamba/cello, and an exceedingly rare mandolin with its original case. The NMM also preserves the 'King Charles IV' violin bow, one of only two bows made in the Stradivari workshop, known to survive. These priceless Stradivari instruments represent 50 years of the master's work and are among the crown jewels of the NMM.

Hundreds of years after Stradivari's death, his violins are still considered by many to be the finest instruments ever made. Whether "Strad," "Stradivari," or "Stradivarius," —his famed name itself conjures up a timeless mystique. And Strad players—some of the world's greatest performers—swear by the violins' sound quality.

Like his creations, Antonio Stradivari was an extraordinary survivor. A force within the 17th and 18th centuries, he lived into his 90's, producing within his workshop more than 1,000 stringed instruments: violins, cellos, guitars, lutes, mandolins, bows, and more. Built to last, but also safeguarded by owner after owner, more than half of those instruments still exist, many in playing condition.

Originally influenced by the great Amati family and Cremonese tradition before him, Stradivari was a brilliant innovator who went on to perfect many aspects of the violin. 'Strads' (as they are called) are still favored for their sound projection, tonal color, and exquisite craftsmanship.

As if harboring some elusive secret recipe, Strads have been endlessly analyzed and researched. And no instrument has been more often copied. They remain the gold standard in the world of stringed instruments.

Back of peghead of NMM's 'Rawlins' guitar with Stradivari signature, 1700 **[more on p. 56]**

Stradivari 'Cutler-Challen' mandolin

Antonio Stradivari (1644–1737)
Cremona, Italy, 1680

Although best known today for his violins, Stradivari made all kinds of stringed instruments.

The NMM's Stradivari mandolin is *one of only two in existence*, and, miraculously, it survives with its original wood case.

Described as "light as a feather," the mandolin's back is made of seven maple ribs. The soundboard is made of spruce and has an intricately carved rose made of pearwood.

Stradivari signed the instrument himself. His handwriting, in ink, appears on the inside of the mandolin: *Antonio Stradiuario in Cremona 1680*.

Amazingly, this *choral mandolino* (as Stradivari referred to this particular model), still has its original neck, though the original peghead was lost in the passage of time. Fortunately, several patterns relating to the mandolin's construction survive in the Museo del Violino in Cremona, Italy, and a faithful peghead was reconstructed by an expert luthier.

This mandolin is referred to now as the 'Cutler-Challen,' named, as Stradivari instruments customarily are, after a particular owner (Challen), musician, or benefactor (Cutler).

NMM 6045
Purchase funds gift of Mr. and Mrs. Richard A. Cutler, 1997

Stradivari 'Harrison' violin

Antonio Stradivari (1644–1737)
Cremona, Italy, 1693

Stradivari—the world's greatest violin maker.

No violin is more famous than a Stradivari. And the National Music Museum is proud to preserve one of the most outstanding produced by the legendary Italian maker.

The NMM's extraordinary 'Harrison' is among the finest of the finest: one of only a half-dozen Stradivari violins to survive with its original neck and pegbox. (Most early violin necks were replaced in the 19th century.)

This has also been called "the greatest concert violin built before 1700." With its elegant, narrowed curves, the 'Harrison' is one of Stradivari's 'long pattern' instruments, introduced in the 1690s. About a centimeter longer than today's violins and designed with a relatively flat arching, this model represents Stradivari's first major innovation and departure from the classic Amati model also made in Cremona.

So highly valued, all Stradivari violins are given names. The NMM's instrument is named after Richard Harrison, an English lawyer and musician who owned it from 1892–1907. The 'Harrison' has lived all over the world in its long and illustrious history of ownership.

Before being purchased by Bob Rawlins as a gift to the NMM in honor of his wife Marge, the 'Harrison' was owned by the great Korean violinist Kyung-Wha Chung—who can be heard and seen playing it in recorded performances from the 1970s.

NMM 3598
Rawlins Fund, 1985

Stradivari 'Rawlins' guitar

Antonio Stradivari (1644–1737)
Cremona, Italy, 1700

NMM 3976
Rawlins Fund, 1985

Stradivari made guitars?

The most famous name in violin making, Antonio Stradivari also built superb guitars. The National Music Museum's 'Rawlins' is *one of only five Stradivari guitars known to still exist.*

Stradivari's signature is on the inside of most of his instruments. On his guitars, his name is immediately visible—inscribed in Latin, with the date, on the back of the guitar's peghead. [See p. 53.]

Stradivari's guitars are not as ornate as many other Italian Baroque guitars. Instead, Stradivari was one of the first makers to highlight the natural beauty of the wood on a guitar, using a spruce top and a lush violin-style figured maple for the back and sides. His decorative details are elegant and restrained.

The circle-and-diamond inlay motif around the soundhole is a signature Stradivari pattern, one he also used on a group of violin-family stringed instruments made for the Spanish court.

The 'Rawlins' guitar has five doubled strings (courses), typical of the Baroque period.

This 'Rawlins' guitar is named in honor of the late Robert and Marjorie Rawlins, whose generous funding made the NMM's purchase of the guitar and the entire Witten-Rawlins Collection possible.

Stradivari 'Fruh' cello

Antonio Stradivari (1644–1737)
Cremona, Italy, 1730

A musical metamorphosis . . .

This remarkable cello was actually first a *viola da gamba* (a bass instrument held between the 'gams'/player's legs) that was crafted in Antonio Stradivari's famed workshop around 1730. Stradivari was in his mid-80's at the time (he lived to be 93!), so it is likely that one of his sons collaborated on the instrument. Nonetheless, the unique carving of the f-holes, the arching, the fine spruce soundboard, and the flat, curly-maple back are telltale Stradivari.

One hundred years later, louder instruments were in demand. Music was moving out of private, aristocratic homes and into public concert halls, where sound had to travel farther. This instrument was updated with a new neck and taller sides, converting it into a cello. The soundboard was extended at the top, but the shape of the *viola da gamba* is still clearly visible.

Fast forward to our time. The instrument is now known as the 'Fruh cello,' named after its most recent former owner, cellist Karl Fruh. A musical masterpiece, the instrument still plays beautifully.

NMM 10845
Gift of Karl B. and Helen Fruh Estate, 2005

Lyre-guitar

François Roudhloff (1781–1849)
Paris, France, ca. 1805–1817

All things ancient Greek and Roman—neoclassical in design—were status symbols in the high society of the late 18th and early 19th centuries. With upright arms like an ancient Greek lyre, this 6-stringed instrument is actually strummed like a guitar. Inlaid with mother-of-pearl, this exquisite lyre-guitar by Parisian maker François Roudhloff could either be played as a musical instrument or simply displayed in the parlor as an object of art.

Southern belle Elizabeth "Lizinka" McKay Campbell Brown Ewell (1820–1872) proudly owned this lyre-guitar. The beautiful daughter of a Tennessee statesman and minister to Russia, Lizinka was pursued by many suitors. She received the lyre-guitar from a naval officer but later became the wife and then widow of a landholder and attaché to the American embassy in Paris. She married again, to her cousin, a Confederate general. When Union forces occupied her Nashville home during the Civil War, she fled, taking care to hide this lyre-guitar away. After her son George Campbell Brown returned from being a prisoner of war, he found the instrument safely stowed beneath some straw in the barn. In 1866, he gave Lizinka's lyre-guitar away, to family-friend Fanny Bayless Willett, who documented the instrument's ownership history.

NMM 3166
Purchase funds gift of Helen Beede Sill and Grace L. Beede, 1982

Chanot ergonomic violin

François Chanot (ca. 1788–1825), Chanot and Lété workshop
Paris, France, ca. 1819

Modern art—or musical instrument? The shock of the Chanot.

The early 19th century was a wildly experimental time across all technological fields, including musical-instrument making. As a naval engineer from a French violin-making family, François Chanot set out to remake the violin.

Boldly rethinking the violin's form, Chanot introduced this asymmetrical model around 1819. He narrowed one of violin's upper shoulders radically so that reaching the higher positions would be easier. He reshaped the violin's lower portion so that it would conform more organically to the space between the player's neck and shoulder.

Chanot's violin made a big splash at its introduction. Critics acknowledged its artistic audacity and praised its sound. But Chanot's futuristic design was ahead of its time. Violinists continued to prefer the traditional form. But many modern-day violin and guitarmakers have adopted Chanot's streamlined soundholes—slot-shaped cutouts—instead of the more complicated historic 'f' shape.

The National Music Museum has one of the most comprehensive collections of rare Chanot stringed instruments, with *five* examples, including *the only surviving Chanot 'ergonomic' violin.*

NMM 14530
Purchase funds gift of Marifran Wohlenberg, 2011

Crocodile-shaped zither (*mì-gyaùng* or *kyam*)

Mon people
Burma, 19th century

The National Music Museum Zoo?

Many of the NMM's most fascinating instruments are related to animals—made from their bones, shells, skins, and more; or decorated with carvings, engravings, or painted images of animals. Some instruments are even constructed to look like specific animals—especially creatures common to a particular culture.

This crocodile-shaped zither was made in Burma (modern Myanmar) in the 19th century. According to the mythology of the ethnic Mon people, a Mon king ordered these instruments to be created in honor of his son, who was once transported by a sacred crocodile.

Decorated with gold paint and colored glass, this carved-wood zither is 31 inches long, has three strings, brass frets, and is plucked with a plectrum. The ivory tuning-peg tips are carved to resemble lotus blossoms.

Zithers date back more than a thousand years in Asia, but the *mì-gyaùng/kyam* fell out of favor by the early 1800's, with the decline of the Mon kingdom.

NMM 2618
Beede Fund, 1979

Peacock-shaped lute (*mayuri*)

Maker unknown
India, 19th century

Strutting its stuff, this plucky peacock-shaped lute is a visitor-favorite in the musical menagerie at the National Music Museum.

Popular in Indian royal courts of the 19th century, the *mayuri* (from the Hindi word for "peacock") is associated with Saraswati, the Hindu goddess of wisdom, creativity, poetry, and music. In more recent history, Sikh musicians in India have revived the playing of the instrument, particularly as an accompaniment to religious music.

To play the *mayuri*, a musician plucks the strings with one hand while drawing a bow across them with the other. Like many Indian stringed instruments, the *mayuri* has melody strings and unplayed 'sympathetic' strings (which vibrate distinctively when the melody stringed are played). The unique sound, resonating within the wooden peacock body, is deep and mellow.

Blue and green—like the peacock species native to India—this lavishly painted *mayuri* features a real peacock beak and tail feathers.

NMM 2903
Purchase funds gift of Edwin and Lydia Downie, 1981

Double chromatic harp

Henry Greenway (1833–1903)
Brooklyn, New York, ca. 1895

Playing difficulty: angel level.

Straight out of New York's Gilded Age at the turn of the 20th century, this opulent two-in-one harp, invented and built by Henry Greenway, is one of only two such instruments known to survive (the other being at the Metropolitan Museum of Art in New York City).

Lavishly encrusted with decorative elements such as gilded plaster grapevines and roses, the harp is made of fine woodwork and brasswork. The instrument's columns, made of birdseye maple, soar winglike to five-and-a-half feet in height—conjoined dramatically in an 'x' at the center.

The harp is strung with two sets of strings: forty-three on the neck to the player's left, grouped like the white keys on a piano; thirty-one to the player's right, grouped like the black keys.

Some records suggest that this double harp was made under the direction of a Chicago touring harpist, Mme. LaRoche, who conceived it as a way to handle the chromatics required by orchestral arrangements.

The harp served just as often as a showpiece of concentrated wealth, in the rarified air of high society.

NMM 5728
Acquisition funds gift of Carole and Bruce Stavens, 1994

Ukulele

José do Espírito Santo (1850–1905)
Honolulu, Hawaii, ca. 1895–1905

Uke can do it.

The ukulele may be as Hawaiian as pineapples, but its origins are actually Portuguese. Maker José do Espírito Santo emigrated from the Portuguese island of Madeira in 1879 with a group of his countrymen to work on Hawaiian sugar plantations. Cabinetmakers by trade, they discovered a demand for musical instruments. As skilled woodworkers with new materials at hand, they developed what came to be called the *ukulele*. Based on Portuguese stringed instruments like the *machete*, the ukulele is basically a scaled-down guitar.

Espírito Santo was the first to advertise sales of ukuleles in 1898. The NMM's very early and remarkably rare Espírito Santo ukulele is just twenty inches long—notably smaller than those made after Espírito Santo's death.

The soundboard is made of *koa*, a native Hawaiian wood. The uke's ribs, fretboard and pineapple-esque headstock are overlaid in beautiful designs, crafted of alternating tropical hardwoods.

Ukuleles achieved popularity and mass production in the United States by the 1910s and have gone through waves of boom and bust. The Internet and indie rock have popularized and legitimized the ukulele as a serious instrument, while spreading its infectious good-energy sound and accessibility to a subculture of new players and fans.

NMM 14680
Purchase funds gift of Marifran Wohlenberg and David L. Rose, 2012

‘New Yorker’ archtop guitar

John D’Angelico (1905–1964)
New York City, 1947

Angelic artisanry.

A son of immigrants from Naples, John D’Angelico began his luthier training at nine, in the workshop of his great-uncle Raphael Ciani, in New York City’s Little Italy. He absorbed Old World practices as he helped make guitars and mandolins. By 1932, he had his own shop in Manhattan where he produced hand-carved archtops (violin-inspired guitars with curved tops—the opposite of ‘flat tops’). He made them in the style of a popular Gibson guitar called the L-5. But it was his own models—the *Excel* and *New Yorker*—which earned him a devoted following among guitarists in the city’s thriving jazz and big-band scene, as well as with country crooners like Chet Atkins. His instruments were (and still are) prized not only for their acoustic qualities but for their beautiful looks.

The sumptuous styling of these instruments reflects the Art Deco designs in architecture and the decorative arts. The *New Yorker* features inlaid mother-of-pearl and D’Angelico’s signature-tailpiece based on the ‘stair-step’ architectural lines of the former New Yorker Hotel. The natural finish highlights the guitar’s smooth curves, arched spruce soundboard, and maple back.

The NMM’s *New Yorker* was custom-made by D’Angelico for young touring musician Mario Bagnoni (1922–2005).

D’Angelico’s ledger books, preserved by the NMM, show a slow trickle of instruments from his storefront—fewer than 1,200 guitars—not mass produced but meticulously handcrafted with Old World care. They are now highly collectible.

NMM 10827
Tony and Bonnie Vinatieri Family Trust, 2005

Guitar Workshop of John D'Angelico and James D'Aquisto

The 'Stradivaris of the American archtop guitar'

Among the greatest of archtop guitar-makers, 20th-century Americans John D'Angelico and James D'Aquisto set the bar for high-end craftsmanship and design. Their instrument-making standard is everywhere evident in their highly prized guitars and in their workshop on display at the National Music Museum. The workbenches, guitar rack, tools, patterns, molds, guitar backs, sides, tops, ledger books, and other artifacts from their legendary original storefront at 40 Kenmare St. in Little Italy, New York City, are testament to the painstaking art of fine lutherie.

From apprentice to master

New Yorker James D'Aquisto (1935–1995) was born into a Sicilian-American family and a culture of fine craftsmanship. He began his apprenticeship in John D'Angelico's Manhattan workshop in 1952. Over the following decades, D'Aquisto mastered his teacher's skills and then went beyond, introducing his own innovative guitar designs. He departed from D'Angelico's basic *Excel* and *New Yorker* styling and created bold new archtop models, including the *Avant Garde*, *Solo*, *Centura*, *Advance*, and *Futura*. He experimented with arching, bracing, bridges, and soundhole design, while modernizing the look of instruments. D'Aquisto's guitars are now even more highly coveted than those of the great D'Angelico.

The contents of the workshop were given to the NMM in memory of guitar-maker, collector, and D'Aquisto-apprentice Paul Gudelsky (1963–1996) by Louise Palazola and Erwin Gudelsky, with additional funding from the Tom & Cindy Lillibridge Fund, 2005, and the Tony and Bonnie Vinatieri Family Trust, 2005.

Les Paul-model electric guitar

Gibson Inc.
Kalamazoo, Michigan, 1952

The golden guitar.

Musician Les Paul (1915–2009) had a profound impact on American pop music and guitar culture. An early advocate for electric instruments and recording technologies, he had a long-standing relationship with the Gibson company that resulted in the design of this signature guitar. The Les Paul model, introduced in 1952, is one of the great classic designs and is still in production today.

The Les Paul model is made from mahogany with a maple veneer. The standard "Goldtop" version is iconic and highly collectible. Famous musicians like Paul McCartney and the Rolling Stones' Keith Richards own and play Goldtops. The NMM's guitar—yet more rare—is not only gold on top, it is finished on all sides in gold metallic lacquer.

This particular guitar also features a rare modified version of the "trapeze" tailpiece-bridge combination patented in the early 1950s by Lester W. Polfuss (a.k.a. Les Paul), which was replaced by a standard bridge in the second year of production.

NMM 5916
Board of Trustees, 1995

Explorer electric guitar

Gibson, Inc.
Kalamazoo, Michigan, 1958/1967

One of the coolest instruments in the NMM's collection is the Explorer guitar, once owned by rock star John Entwistle.

It's easy to forget how radical this guitar design was when it was introduced by Gibson in the late 1950s. Literally cutting-edged and angular—nothing like the traditional curved guitar—the Explorer was one of a set of futuristic-looking electric guitars that included the iconic 'Flying V.'

Trailblazers ahead of their time, Explorers were not popular right away (not until the ascent of hard rock in the 1970s). They were discontinued in 1959, just a year after their introduction. During the 1960s, some of the original 1958 Explorer bodies were finally furnished with modern electronics and fittings. The NMM's Explorer is likely one of the last made, sold in 1967.

The Explorer is a six-string guitar with a signature 'hockey-stick'-shaped headstock. Its solid body is made from the light-colored African hardwood *limba*, which the Gibson Company called *korina*. Lighter in weight than mahogany, korina is said to produce a 'brighter' tone. Among collectors, scarce korina guitars from the Golden Age of electric guitars are the holy grail of instruments and are exceptionally valuable.

This Explorer is one of the NMM's celebrity-related instruments. It was previously owned by John Entwistle (1944–2002), of the famed British rock band *The Who*. Considered by many to be one of the greatest rock bass-guitarists who ever lived, Entwistle was also an avid and very discerning guitar collector.

NMM 14720
Board of Trustees, 2013

Johnny Cash guitar

RG&G Musical Instruments, Inc.
(Grammer Guitar Company)
Nashville, Tennessee, 1966–1967

The life story of country-music superstar and American folk icon Johnny Cash (1932–2003) could be told through his guitars: the Sears Roebuck model his mother played for him when he was a boy; the first guitar he bought—an unbranded model—when he was an American serviceman in Germany; his many beloved Martin dreadnoughts.

Two of the celebrity instruments at the National Music Museum are guitars associated with the legendary 'man in black.'

This flat-top acoustic guitar is by the Grammer Company, founded by Johnny's friend, country artist Billy Grammer. Stylized to capture a classic country-western look, the guitar has a spruce soundboard with Brazilian rosewood ribs and back, and a mahogany neck. The "Johnny Cash" signature is rendered in inlaid mother-of-pearl between the 4th and 13th frets.

The NMM is also home to the guitar now known as the 'Bon Aqua.' Intimately connected with the last 30 years of Cash's life, the 1971 Martin D-28 guitar was his instrument of choice at his beloved farm near Bon Aqua, Tennessee, where he went to compose new music and decompress from touring. Created in the 1930s, the D-28 dreadnought model's robust bass sound made it a popular choice of country artists since its introduction.

NMM 14717
Anonymous gift, 2013

June Carter Cash's 'Hummingbird' guitar

Gibson, Inc.
Kalamazoo, Michigan, 1967

"Keep on the Sunny Side"
— American song classic popularized by the Carter Family

This sunny 1967 acoustic guitar by the Gibson company is one of the NMM's celebrity instruments, belonging originally to the "first lady of country music," June Carter Cash (1929–2003).

A member of the Carter Family—folk-music royalty and some of the earliest country recording artists—and second wife of the legendary Johnny Cash, June Carter Cash was an accomplished singer-songwriter and musician in her own right. A Grammy-Award winner and lifelong Nashville performer, she played guitar, banjo, autoharp, and harmonica.

This 'Hummingbird' model was one of Carter Cash's favorite guitars. Its big resonant tone and projecting power made it ideal for voice accompaniment and showmanship. She was still playing this guitar in 1999 when she made her late-career album *Press On*.

Introduced in 1960 and embraced also by the likes of Keith Richards and Gram Parsons, the 'Hummingbird' model was Gibson's first square-shouldered dreadnought. This elegant flat-top guitar is made of spruce and mahogany, with a Brazilian rosewood fingerboard and mother-of-pearl inlays. It was named for the image of a hummingbird that appears on the transparent red celluloid pickguard.

NMM 10768
André and Kay Marcum Larson Fund, 2004

Elvis Presley guitar

C. F. Martin & Co.
Nazareth, Pennsylvania, 1975

The guitar that got 'all shook up.'

The King of Rock and Roll, Elvis Presley (1935–1977), was a consummate showman. His guitars were his rhythm instruments, dance partners, and props. In his later years of touring, he would often arrange to throw one of his guitars up in the air during a show, staging a crew member out in the audience ready to catch it. On Valentine's Day 1977 in Tampa, Florida, the timing of the stunt went slightly awry, and the valuable Martin D-35 guitar crashed to the ground instead. Seizing the crowd-pleasing moment, Presley presented the slightly splintered instrument to a star-struck, ecstatic fan.

The guitar is now Elvis history.

The Martin company's big D-size guitars (D for "dreadnought," after the large WWI-era British battleships) were among Elvis's go-to guitars. The D-35's booming bass tone makes it an ideal rhythm guitar for many genres, particularly country, bluegrass, and rock. Made of spruce, rosewood and mahogany, the D-35 is a classic Martin flat top.

Elvis played the NMM's Martin D-35 guitar in 29 concerts between September 1976 and the February 1977 concert—that is, in his final year of touring. Just seven months later, he would be dead.

"Love me tender," sang Presley, immortally. The National Music Museum will always preserve this special guitar as is—flaws and all.

NMM 14715
Anonymous gift, 2013

Dobro slide steel guitar

Dopyera Brothers, Inc.
Chicago, Illinois, 1978

People often call any resonator guitar a "Dobro." But this is the *real* thing—made by the Do(pyera) Bro(thers) of Chicago.

Slovakian immigrant and inventor John Dopyera (1893–1988) patented a design for resonator guitars in 1927, when he was with the National String Instrument Corporation. Seeking to make acoustic guitars louder, audible above the drums and horns in early twentieth-century dance bands, Dopyera replaced the wooden soundboard top of a guitar with a vibrating metal cone (or, 'resonator'). The metal on metal of guitar strings and cone not only increased the instrument's volume but created a distinctive new sound.

Dopyera left National, and with his brothers Emile, Robert, and Louis, formed the Dobro Manufacturing Company in 1929. ("Dobro" also happens to mean "goodness" in Slovak.) The firm made the guitar yet louder, with a bowl-shaped resonator under a circular 'spider web' cover.

Electric guitars eventually surpassed resonator guitars in volume and versatility, but resonators had found their niche. The galloping, metallic "Dobro" sound is still a staple of blues and bluegrass.

The NMM's stunning, fully nickel-plated Dobro was made as a gift for the donor, at the request of the Dopyera brothers' niece. Though recently retired, the brothers created it from one of the last guitar bodies in their workshop.

NMM 10111
Gift of Pamela D. Schmidt and Western International Music, Inc., 2002

Keyboard
INSTRUMENTS

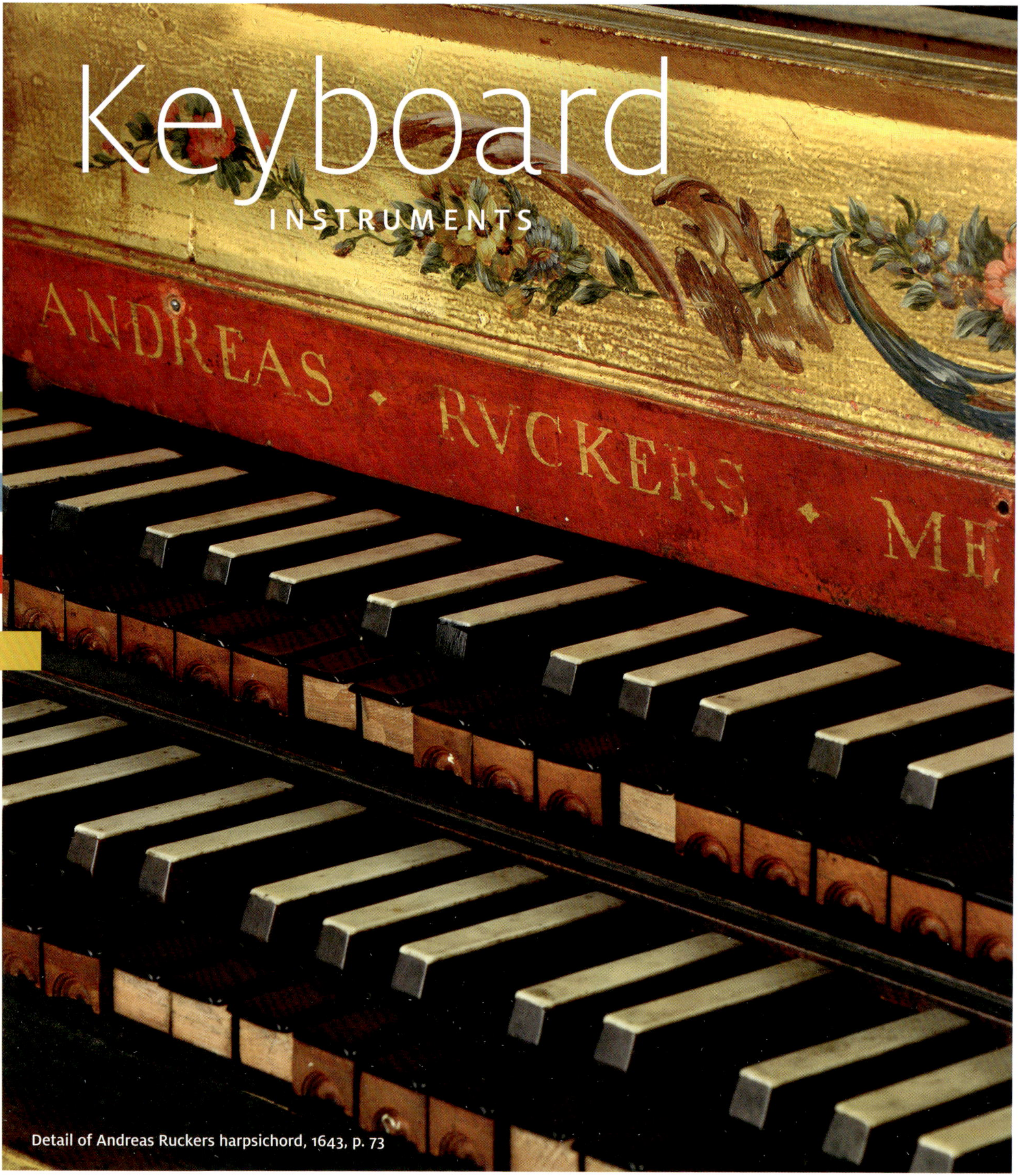

Detail of Andreas Ruckers harpsichord, 1643, p. 73

Ruckers harpsichord

Andreas Ruckers the Elder (1579–ca. 1653)
Antwerp, Belgium, 1643

The 'Stradivaris' of harpsichords.

The Ruckers family dynasty dominated keyboard-making from about 1580 through 1670. Their famed harpsichords were highly valued for their sound quality and were widely imitated and exported throughout Europe and even the New World.

Like almost all surviving double-manual Flemish harpsichords, this instrument was altered in the 18th century. The two original keyboards were discarded, and the case was enlarged to accommodate new keyboards with more keys.

This harpsichord is also a spectacular canvas of changing tastes in art and interior design. The soundboard, original and dated 1643, is painted with whimsical flowers, fruits, birds, bugs, and even shrimp. In contrast, the painting on the inside of the harpsichord's lid is dark and dramatic. Scenes from Greek mythology—featuring Orpheus, Amphion, and more—symbolize the power of music [See Contents, p. 5].

In the 19th century, this harpsichord's case was further embellished with painted garlands, flowers, and music-playing cherubs.

Fewer than 100 Ruckers' family instruments exist, and the NMM is one of the few places in the world that preserves both standard models of Ruckers harpsichords—single-manual and double-manual.

NMM 10000
Purchase funds gift of Margaret L. Sletwold Estate and Arne B. and Jeanne F. Larson Fund, 2000

Neapolitan harpsichord

Maker unknown
Naples, Italy, ca. 1530

A time machine and true survivor—the earliest known playable harpsichord.

Imagine a musical instrument built not long after Columbus' voyages—from the time of Michelangelo, Martin Luther, and Henry the VIII—and still able to make beautiful music some 500 years later.

The 'Neapolitan' harpsichord is one of the crown jewels of the National Music Museum's collections and one of the world's most historic keyboard instruments.

The instrument is unsigned, and the maker is not known, but the keyboard construction is very similar to work done by artisans in Naples in the early 1500s. Much like the finest guitars and mandolins of the Italian Renaissance, the Neapolitan's soundboard features an intricately carved 'rose' soundhole.

The harpsichord is made of maple, its soundboard of spruce, and its keys are of ebony and boxwood. It can be taken out of its elaborately painted green case to be played, or played with the case remaining on it.

With such fine craftsmanship, materials, and longevity, the Neapolitan required only minimal restoration at the NMM. It has since been played and recorded—transporting listeners back to the early 16th century.

NMM 14408
Purchase funds gift of the William Selz Estate; Clifford and LaVonne Graese; and Rawlins Fund, 2009

Carved soundhole rose

Neapolitan harpsichord inside its case

Van Everbroeck harpsichord

Gommaar van Everbroeck (ca. 1603/4–ca. 1666)
Antwerp, Belgium, 1659

"Reader, neither the author nor the work requires your praise: the work glorifies the author; and the author [glorifies] the work."

—Translation of Latin text under lid of harpsichord

This is the only surviving harpsichord by Gommaar van Everbroeck, one of the great 17th-century Flemish makers. All the more remarkable, this instrument has survived essentially unaltered, musically and decoratively (in contrast to the Ruckers harpsichord on p. 73). It even has its original bone keyboard.

Antwerp harpsichords were made to delight the ears *and* eyes. Their soundboards are elaborately painted, and the inside of their lids were traditionally decorated with woodblock-printed papers.

Van Everbroeck likely worked in the shop of Joannes Ruckers, brother of Andreas, who made the NMM's double-manual harpsichord [pp. 72–73]. The Van Everbroeck's soundboard was probably painted by the same anonymous artist who painted soundboards for Joannes Ruckers.

This harpsichord was made six years after the death of Andreas Ruckers the Elder (1653) and in the same year as Andreas Ruckers the Younger's death (1659). Still working in the Ruckers' shadow, Van Everbroeck may be using his bold Latin inscription to stake his individuality and independence, as if to say, 'This harpsichord may not be a Ruckers, but it's a *Van Everbroeck*—great in its own right.'

NMM 3985
Rawlins Fund, 1986

Thÿm grand piano

Anton Martin Thÿm (active 1813–1821)
Vienna, Austria, ca. 1815

A piano with all the bells and whistles—almost!

Long before our era of electronically generated special effects, keyboard makers like Anton Martin Thÿm were busy creating ways to imitate the then highly popular sounds of percussion-heavy Turkish Janissary bands.

'Janissary pianos,' like this one, were outfitted with extra pedals to activate the instrument's special effects, mimicking the sounds of other musical instruments—including the bassoon, harp, bells, and a loud bass drum. Additional pedals control the *una corda* (the "soft pedal"), the dampers, and both a strong and medium moderator (a layer of leather brought between the hammers and strings to mute the sound).

This 6-octave piano can be played loudly with thunderous accents from the seventh pedal (bells and drum) or with extraordinarily soft effects, by using combinations of the soft pedal, harp, and dampers.

The Thÿm's case is itself an art object, made of purpleheart wood, inlaid with ebony and fruitwood, and covered with inked drawings of landscapes, lovers, tiny portraits, flowers, and the signature *Anton Martin Thÿm/No. 94, Vienne*. The piano's legs are carved figures of Nubian servants, subjects of the 19th-century Ottoman Empire. Are they holding up the piano—or covering their ears at its loud din?

NMM 3587
Rawlins Fund, 1985. Restoration funds gift of Stella Anker, 1985

Swiss house organ

Josef Looßer (1749–1822)
Lüppfertsweil, Gemeind Cappel,
St. Gall, Switzerland, 1786

One of the most colorful instruments—in appearance and history—at the NMM is this historic Swiss house organ, built in 1786 by Josef Looßer. It is the only 6-stop organ by this master craftsman known to survive.

Originally intended to be installed in private homes, these organs were used to accompany the singing of sacred songs, at a time when music was banned in many Swiss churches. Decorated with folk painting and trimmed with gilded rococo carving, the organ reflects the style of Switzerland's Toggenburger region in the 18th century.

House organs like this are rarely found outside of Switzerland. This organ, however, was acquired a century ago by a British countess, who kept it for years in her villa in Assisi, Italy. Later transported to England, the instrument was found to have woodworm damage and was professionally restored in the late 1980s. To maintain its 18th-century authenticity, the organ was not electrified. Its sound is still produced the old-fashioned way: wind pressure is supplied by a bellows, which is filled when the organist pushes down on the pedal. All but 30 of the organ's 294 pipes are original, one of them inscribed with the maker's name and date. In 1990, the NMM acquired the organ, pledging to continue to preserve it and its unique history.

NMM 4897
Purchase funds gift of Margaret Ann and Hubert H. Everist, 1990